Get Financial Aid and Go to College

Everything you want to know to get the funds you need and succeed in college

by James Patrick Hilliard

Published by Hilliard Media, Hesperia, CA
hilliardmedia.us

Library of Congress Control Number: 2025903394

ISBN-13: 979-8-9926961-1-0 Paperback

ISBN-13: 979-8-9926961-4-1 e-Book

ISBN-13: 979-8-9926961-7-2 Audiobook

10 9 8 7 6 5 4 3 2 1

First Edition

Printed in USA

Table of Contents

Chapter 3 - Services for Students with Disabilities

Chapter 4 - Military and Veterans Financial Aid

Chapter 5 - International Students Financial Aid

Appendices

Introduction

Many people don't attempt to go to college because they think that they can't, or don't know that they can, get financial aid. They may see getting a degree as an endeavor bigger than they are capable of achieving, or they might not know how to go about it. Just thinking about it may be overwhelming to some and they may simply want to give up before they even try. These thoughts can be laid to rest.

No one has to think that they are incapable of going to school, getting a degree, or receiving financial aid. The first step is to believe in yourself, and the second step is to simply try. You will be surprised how easy it is and how many people are there to help you succeed.

Every journey, no matter how long, is made up of small steps. Over time, these small steps will add up and before you know it you will be at your destination, achieving your dreams and goals.

Getting a strong education is one of the greatest tools a person can have on their side. The old saying "knowledge is power" is very true. The more educated you become, the more you understand the world around you, what makes things the way they are, and how you can apply your given talents to better your life!

As the author, I encourage anyone to go to school. It doesn't matter if you come from a disadvantaged background, a poor household, have no family, have no money, have no friends, or are disabled. Many people have said that their lives were pointless and directionless and that school saved them. Once they started going to school, they started meeting people that had similar interests, who wanted to better themselves, and before they knew it, had friends, a sense of purpose, confidence, and were doing something meaningful with their lives.

The only surefire way to fail at something is to not try. By trying, you have nothing to lose and everything to gain. The information presented in this book will show you how you can receive financial aid and enroll in college – step by step – and hopefully change your life!

So, give it a try!

Chapter 1

Financial Aid

Who Can Get Financial Aid?

Almost anyone can get financial aid!

That is, anyone who is enrolled in school and attending classes can receive financial aid of some sort, provided that you have not yet exhausted what you are qualified to receive and not defaulted on any student loans, making you ineligible, although you may still be able to have your cost of tuition waved by submitting a BOGG application (See Grants).

Money is allotted only for those who are attending, or plan to attend, school. If you successfully apply for financial aid, as outlined in this book, you may be able to receive aid prior to attending classes so that you do not have to pay any enrollment fees up front. That's right! You may be able to enroll in classes without having to pay anything up front. However, you will not be able to receive financial aid if you do not enroll in and attend classes. You must be enrolled in at least half-time status to receive student loans; however, you can receive grants if you enroll in as little as 1 unit if your EFC is 0. (See EFC below.)

Requirements for Receiving Financial Aid

There are two initial requirements that have to be met in order for you to receive financial aid. First, you have to be enrolled in classes with at least half-time status (for student loans). Second, you have to have applied for financial aid and accepted either a grant or a loan. Usually you will have to sign some kind of agreement to accept the responsibilities of the loan, such as a promissory note, if it is a loan and not a grant. Loans differ from grants in that everyone can get loans.

Requirements

When applying for financial aid, a deciding factor in determining whether or not you will receive grants or loans, and how much of each you will get, is what information you provide when filling out the FAFSA (Free Application for Federal Student Aid).

Each school has different requirements, which change each year, and vary by state and type of school. Various factors are taken into consideration, such as: your parent's income based on their income taxes, whether or not both parents work, how many people live in your household, how many people in your household attend college, your parent's ages, what state you live in, and the value or your current assets.

EFC (Expected Family Contribution)

A unique formula is used to combine this information and determine a score called an EFC (Expected Family Contribution). The lower your EFC score is the better chance you have at receiving a grant. Although family incomes up to $50,000, or even up to $100,000, can receive a grant, generally the majority of grants go to families with yearly incomes of less than $30,000 depending on the number of people in your household, the information you provide on the FAFSA, and what your EFC is.

The ratio of people in a household compared to the income of the household, as well as the number of people in the household in college, plays a major role in determining your EFC score. If there are a lot of people in a household, but few or none are in college, your EFC will be lower.

Independent vs. Dependent Status

When filling out the FAFSA for financial aid, you will have to provide either your parent's or your tax information, depending on whether you are considered to be an independent or dependent student. The amount of funds you can receive may be determined by this factor. Who can claim you on their taxes and where the student lives doesn't matter.

Independent Student

You are considered to be an independent student if you meet any of the following criteria:

- You are 24 years of age or older.
- You are married.

- You are enrolled in a master's or doctorate program.
- You are an orphan or ward of the state.
- You are a veteran of the U.S. armed services.
- You have children that receive more than half of their support from you.
- You have dependents other than your children or spouse who live with you.

Note: *Because of the age requirement above, many students between the ages of 18 and 23 don't qualify for financial aid even though they are living on their own and not being claimed on their parent's taxes as a dependent. If this pertains to you and your income is within qualifying limits you can complete a Change of Income form and submit it to the financial aid office. This will replace your previous income information on file with your current income and may make you eligible for aid.*

Dependent Student

A dependent student must use his or her parents' income tax information to determine eligibility for student aid. Sometimes this may disqualify a student from receiving aid. You are considered a dependent student if you do not meet any of the criteria listed above.

Enrollment Status

The amount of units you are enrolled in determines whether your enrollment status is full or half-time. Each class that you enroll in will be worth a certain number of units upon completion of the class. For example, a biology class may be a 3-unit class. If you enroll in two 3-unit classes, you will be enrolled in a total of 6 units. If you enroll in four 3-unit classes or three 4-unit classes, you will be enrolled in 12 units. The number of classes you enroll in doesn't matter in determining your status. It is the number of units you are enrolled in that determines your status. Each school determines differently how half or full-time status is defined.

Half-time enrollment status means that you are enrolled in at least 6 units.

This is the minimum requirement to receive student loans. As mentioned earlier this requirement does not apply to grants if your EFC is 0.

Full-time enrollment status means that you are enrolled in at least 12 units. In some cases, graduate level classes are weighed more heavily than undergraduate level classes therefore enrolling in 8 or 9 units can be considered full time status.

There are some exceptions to this rule however. For example, graduate level classes are weighed more heavily than undergraduate level classes. Therefore, enrollment in 2 graduate level classes (at least 8 units) may constitute full-time status and enrollment in 1 graduate level class (at least 4 units) may constitute half-time status.

Also, at some schools, enrollment in 6 units during a summer session may constitute full-time status. Likewise, enrollment in 3 units during a summer session may constitute half-time status. This is because summer sessions are shorter in length and, as a result, classes tend to be longer in hours and meet more times per week.

What Kind of Financial Aid is Available?

Loans

Loans are borrowed money, which means that they have to be paid back. Generally, as long as you continue to be enrolled in at least half-time status, loans are not due to be paid back until 6 months after you cease to be enrolled in school or drop below at least half-time status. You will have to sign a promissory note in order to accept the loan. This agreement is a legally binding contract that explains the details of the loan.

Stafford Loan (Direct Loan)

As of 2010-11, the way Stafford Loans were funded has changed. Stafford Loans, also called Direct Loans, were funded in the past by private lenders. Now, these loans are funded directly by the federal government. Therefore, at the time this book was published, the following Stafford Loan information is being included for those who have had them in the past.

The main type of loan is known as the Stafford Loan, or Direct Loan. There are 2 types of Stafford loan programs, those offered by the federal government and those offered by private lenders.

Loans offered by the government are offered through what is called the Federal Direct Student Loan Program (FDSLP). These include "direct loans", which are administered by "direct lending institutions", and are issued directly to students and/or their parents.

Other loans are offered through what is called the Family Federal Education Loan Program (FFELP). These loans are offered by private lenders, such as banks, credit unions, and savings & loan associations, and are guaranteed by the federal government against default.

If you attend a school that is considered a "direct lending institution" you will receive loans directly from the federal government and not from private lenders. (studentaid.gov, 2024)

The Stafford Loan can be either subsidized or unsubsidized.

Subsidized Loans

Subsidized loans are loans whose interest is paid by the government while you are continuing education and enrolled in school. The interest accrued while you are enrolled and attending classes is not payable by you. However, you will be responsible for any interest accrued after ceasing education.

Unsubsidized Loans

Unsubsidized loans are loans whose interest accrued while you are enrolled and continuing your education is not paid by the government. You are responsible to pay this interest. However, you are not obligated to pay this interest while enrolled in school and attending classes. If you elect not to pay this interest while attending classes, it will simply be added to the loan balance.

The Perkins Loan

The Perkins loan is the best type of federal loan available and is offered to students with exceptional financial need. Unlike other loans, it is offered by the school's financial aid department, a campus-based loan, based on a limited pool of funds. It is a subsidized loan and offers better cancellation provisions than the Stafford and PLUS loans.

The PLUS Loan

The PLUS loan is a loan offered to parents to pay for costs of undergraduate students. As of July 1, 2006 graduate and professional students are allowed to borrow PLUS loans to pay for their educational expenses as well.

Plus loans are based on your parent's credit and offered through the Department of Education. Parents must go through the same process when applying as the student does. The difference is the approval is based on credit, not need.

Grants

Grants are funds that you do not have to pay back. Grants can be in the form of money, book vouchers, tuition waivers, and stipends. Whether you receive a grant, or not, is usually based on your income, level of need, and other factors.

The following are grant programs offered through the federal government:

The Pell Grant

The most common type of grant is the federal Pell grant. This grant is available to eligible half and full-time students and can be applied for any time after January 1st for the subsequent Fall semester. Awards range from $400 to $5600 depending on the year, as federal limits change each year, and the amount of the award is based on need and number of units you are enrolled in. You must be a US citizen or eligible non-citizen to receive this type of grant.

Academic Competitiveness Grant (ACG)

The Academic Competitiveness Grant is available to first and second year students who are eligible to receive the federal Pell grant and have been enrolled in a rigorous secondary academic program, as defined by the DOE. Award amounts for first year students are $750 and $1300 for second year students. To receive this grant, you must also meet the following criteria:

- be a US citizen or eligible non-citizen
- first year award recipients must be attending college for the first time
- second year award recipients must have maintained a cumulative GPA of 3.0 or higher during your first year of college

Supplemental Education Opportunity Grant (SEOG)

The Federal Supplemental Education Opportunity Grant is available to qualifying students who are eligible to receive the federal Pell grant. Awards are granted on a first-come first-serve basis up to a maximum of $2000 per year and are based on need. Students with the highest need and lowest EFC are given priority. The SEOG program is a campus based program, which means that funding is limited to the amount of funds that each campus offers.

Work Study

Work study is a grant offered to students who have completed a FAFSA and are eligible to receive financial aid. The FWS allows you to earn a portion of your educational expenses through employment either at the school you are attending or through community service opportunities. You can search and apply for jobs online via the financial aid website. Average awards are $3,000 per school year. You must be enrolled in at least 6 or more units during the fall, winter, and spring semesters.

The following are grant programs offered through the state of California:

Board of Governors Grant (BOGG)

The BOGG, also known as the Promise Grant, will waive the cost of tuition. To receive the BOGG you must qualify by one of 3 of the following methods:

Method 1: Special Classification

You are eligible if you are:

- receiving a form of General Assistance
- receiving SSI or SSP
- a dependent of a disabled veteran
- a recipient or a child of a recipient of the Congressional Medal of Honor
- a dependent of a victim of the 9/11/01 terrorist attack
- a dependent of a deceased law enforcement or fire suppression personnel

Method 2: Household Size and Total Family Income

You are eligible if your total income is less than the amounts indicated, based on family size:

Family Size	Income in $	Family Size	Income in $
1	16,335	5	39,255
2	22,065	6	44,985
3	27,795	7	50,715
4	33,525	8	56,445

Each additional family member - add $5,730

Method 3: Need/Expected Family Contribution

You are eligible if, after completing a FAFSA, your Expected Family Contribution (EFC) demonstrates the minimum need threshold, established annually.

Note: *You may receive the BOGG regardless of whether you are in default of student loans or have reached your aggregate limit for financial aid.*

Cal Grant

The Cal Grant is offered by the state of California and is administered by the California Student Aid Commission (CSAC). It is available only to California residents attending a college or university in California. The application deadline is March 2nd for the following academic year and you must complete a FAFSA and a GPA verification prior to the application deadline (CAL GRANT, 2010).

The Cal Grant is based on academic GPA, need, income, residency, as well as other criteria. There are two types of Cal Grants: competitive and entitlement. You are guaranteed an entitlement Cal Grant if you meet the minimum qualifications and one of the following four criteria:

- You are currently a high school senior, or
- You are within one year of graduation or completion of your GED, or
- You are transferring from a community college to a 4-year university, or
- You have met need and income limitations according to your completed FAFSA

Competitive Cal Grants are a limited number of awards for which you are competing. This Cal Grant has a September 2nd application deadline.

There are three different Cal Grants offered. Cal Grant A, B, and C.

Cal Grant A is for students who are attending a four-year college or university. If you are awarded the Cal Grant A and are attending a community college, you can place your award on reserve status until you attend a four-year college or university.

Cal Grant B is for students who are attending either a California Community College or a four-year college or university.

Cal Grant C is for students who are enrolled in an occupational/technical, or certificate program.

Cal Grant awards vary in amounts and are based on the type of Cal Grant, the type of institution you are attending, and your cost of attendance.

Note: *When submitting your GPA verification for the Cal Grant, you must have completed 24 degree applicable/transferable units, whether from college or high school.*

Book Vouchers

This type of aid is offered to students who are eligible to receive the federal Pell grant. Book vouchers are deducted from your Pell grant award and redeemed to cover the cost of books.

Tuition Waivers

Tuition waivers pay the cost of tuition and are offered to students who are eligible to receive financial aid. This usually consists of the unit cost of the classes.

Stipends

A stipend is an award offered to eligible students in the form of a salary complimented by other benefits, such as accommodations, accreditation, food, and instruction in exchange for work performed, such as an apprenticeship or internship. Stipend salaries are generally lower in comparison for the type of job performed, because of the complimentary benefits obtained. Monies paid to graduate students by Universities are usually referred to as stipends.

Parking Permits

A parking permit gives you the privilege to park on campus. Without one you may be cited and have to pay a fine. Normally a parking decal must be purchased at full price. However, if you purchase an Associated Students card, which allows you to receive various benefits, the cost of the parking decal may be significantly reduced. Students with disabilities can sometimes receive a parking decal at no cost.

Preparatory Test Vouchers

Another voucher that the financial aid offers is a preparatory test voucher. This voucher will cover the cost of taking a preparatory test in order to get into a particular degree program. The financial aid office will usually allow one voucher per year.

Scholarships

Scholarships are awards from various philanthropies to students who apply for them. They usually pertain to your major area of study. For example, Microsoft may award a number of scholarships of a certain dollar amount each year to students who plan on getting a degree in computer science. This money does not have to be paid back.

Military and Veterans Benefits

For information on military and veterans' benefits, see Chapter 4 Military and Veterans Financial Aid.

What Expenses Will Financial Aid Cover?

As mentioned previously, financial aid comes in many forms and can cover the cost of enrolling in classes, books, tuition, tests, room & board, parking permits, and other expenses associated with going to school, depending on the type of financial aid you receive.

Extra Money to Cover Your Expenses (Hidden Secrets)

The majority of students don't realize that they can get additional funds to cover the costs of medical bills, auto repairs, dental expenses, and other costs, such as the need for a new computer, for example, to be able to complete audio or video editing assignments. This is my hidden secret that I discovered from years of going to school and experience dealing with the financial aid office.

Although the school has determined a budget for you to cover the cost of attending school, it doesn't calculate in other unforeseen expenses that arise in emergency situations in life, such as the need for a root canal at the dentist, a visit to the hospital after being in an accident, or your car breaking down. You can have the school pay for these things by way of reimbursement. Keep in mind that they are still part of your loan and will eventually have to be paid back when you go into loan repayment.

You will need to provide receipts for the expenses that you wish to be reimbursed for, which means you will have to pay for them out of pocket first. You will also have to provide a written explanation as to why you need to have your loan budget increased to cover these expenses or why it is necessary for you to get a new computer to complete your school work, for example.

When you meet with a loan counselor to increase your budget, you will provide him or her with receipts and an explanation of the reason for being reimbursed. The loan counselor will review the information you provided and will make a determination to increase your budget or not. If you are successful, the school will send you a check for the amount that you requested.

It is recommended that you sit down with a loan counselor first and honestly discuss the expenses that you will apply for to be reimbursed, to get a sense of what will be considered and what won't.

Financial Aid Limits

Annual Loan Limits

Annual loan limits are the maximum amount of loans a student can borrow on a yearly basis. Loan limits vary by educational level and other factors.

Annual loan limits by educational tier:

- See Appendix A

Aggregate Loan Limits

Aggregate limits are the maximum amount of loans a student can borrow over their academic lifetime. These represent the cumulative total of all various types of student loans that a student has had over his or her lifetime, including undergraduate, graduate, and post-graduate level tiers.

Aggregate loan limits over time by educational tier:

- See Appendix B

Professional schools, such as legal or medical schools, may offer higher aggregate loan limits, as they are costlier to attend.

Although aggregate limits are the cumulative total of loan amounts allowed to borrow, this total can fluctuate if the amount of loans borrowed is paid off or lowered by making payments. In other words, if a student reaches their maximum amount of allowable loans and then pays off some or all of them, the student may be eligible again to receive the amount of available loans.

Pell Grant Limits

The amount of Pell grants awarded to students has been increasing each year due to government funding approval.

Annual Pell grant limits:

- See Appendix C

Loan Repayment

Grace Period

The loan repayment grace period for Stafford loans is 6 months after graduation, or 6 months after you either stop attending school or drop below half-time enrollment status. Half-time enrollment status is the level of enrollment you must hold to stay in deferment.

Some loans have extended grace periods, such as the Perkins loan, which can offer a grace period up to 9 months. For PLUS loans the repayment period begins when the loan is fully disbursed, and the first payment is due within 60 days. However, Graduate students and parents of Graduate students can defer payments on a PLUS loan up to 6 months after the loan has been fully disbursed.

Payment Term

Loan repayment may be different for each type of loan. Usually the payment term is 10-years. What this means is that the amount you owe on student loans is broken up into payments such that the balance will be paid off in full within 10 years. Likewise, your monthly payment will be based on this term. For example, if you owe $60,000 in student loans, your monthly payment based on the 10-year term would be $500. That's $60,000 ÷ 120 months (10 years at 12 months per year) = $500.

Although 10 years is the standard repayment term, longer terms of up to 30 years are available depending on the amount you owe.

Interest Rate

Student loan interest rates vary by the type of loan and date when the loan was taken out. When a student loan is in deferment, any interest is capitalized, meaning that the interest is added onto the principle balance.

- See Appendix D for loan interest rates.

Deferment

Student loans are considered in deferment when payment of them is postponed while you are attending school. Student loans can also stay in deferment after you have finished attending school and are out of the grace period. See below.

Postponement Options

After you have graduated, or ceased to attend school at half-time status or above, you will have at least 6 months before you are required to begin making payment on your student loans, although you are free to make payments anytime during your grace period. If you are unable to make payments on your student loans, there are a few options available to you from the Department of Education (DOE) to help you manage your debt.

Student loans offer 6 years of postponement in two different methods. If you are having a hardship in your life and simply can't make your payments, you can fill out a Forbearance Request Form and postpone, delay the payment date, or reduce your monthly payment for up to 3 years. You can also fill out a Deferment Request Form and postpone your payments for another 3 years. That's a total of 6 years of deferment after you have gone into loan repayment.

Restructure of Payments

Another option is to request a restructure of payments. You will have to fill out another form for this. Sometimes the DOE will reduce your monthly payments based on your income and ability to pay. In some instances, you will be allowed to make a payment as low as $5 a month.

Loan Consolidation

Another option for postponing loan repayment is consolidation. Consolidating your loans is a method of combining all of your eligible student loans into a single monthly payment through the William D. Ford Consolidation Program. In doing so all of your deferment options are reset. To do this, contact the DOE.

If you consolidate your student loans, your previous loans will appear as paid off and a new loan will appear on your credit report.

Loan Forgiveness Programs

The Public Service Loan Forgiveness Program (PSLF) offers cancellation of the remaining balance of any student loans not in default after 120 on-time payments have been made. This means that if you have a student loan and you are employed full-time as a public service employee during the time that the 120 payments are made and at the time of the loan cancellation, the remaining balance of your student loans can be cancelled, or discharged, and you will no longer be obligated to pay them.

There are other loan forgiveness programs available, such as the APLE (Assumption Program of Loans for Education) program, which offers loan forgiveness after 4 years as an instructor at a low income school. This program is offered only in California. Similar programs may be offered by other states.

Loan Cancellation (Discharge)

Under certain circumstances you may be able to have your student loans discharged. This means that your loans will be cancelled and you will no longer be responsible to pay them. In some instances, you may even be eligible to receive a refund of payments you've made on your student loans. There are several methods of cancellation, each pertaining to a different circumstance. They are, discharge due to:

- Death.
- Total and Permanent Disability (TPD).

- School closing and inability to complete program.
- Inability to benefit (False Certification).
- School owing your lender a refund.
- Fraud – your signature was forged on loan documents.

If you are successful at canceling your student loans, any adverse actions reported on your credit report pertaining to the student loans can be removed.

Default

If you fail to make payment on your loans as scheduled in your promissory note, which sets forth your payment terms, you are considered to be in default. Defaulting on your student loans can have severe consequences, such as:

- You will be ineligible to receive any student loans.
- Your loan payments can be deducted from your paycheck (garnishment).
- You will incur late fees and have to pay collection costs.
- National credit bureaus can be notified and your credit rating diminished.
- Your income tax refunds can be applied to offset your debt.
- You can be sued in court.

Loan Information

The DOE keeps track of all of your student loans in a database called the National Student Loan Database, or NSLDS. This information consists of the type of loans, disbursed amounts, monthly payment, principle, interest, originator of the loans, and the dates when they were initiated. This information is available to students to view any time at nsldsfap.ed.gov and is a helpful way for you to keep track of your debt.

The Financial Aid Process

There are a few steps that need to be taken in order to apply for financial aid successfully.

The FAFSA

The first thing to do is to complete a FAFSA (Free Application for Federal Student Aid). This can be done online or via a paper application. The quickest and easiest way is to apply online at fafsa.gov. You will have to create a PIN number to access and fill out the online form and for future logins at the website.

While filling out the FAFSA, you will be asked to provide some personal information, such as name, address, social security number, tax and income information, what schools you are considering attending (usually you can provide four different schools), whether you will be attending full or half-time, whether or not you have registered with selective service, etc. Once submitted, this information will be sent to the DOE (Department of Education), which will automatically determine your loan and grant eligibility based on the information you provided. The DOE will provide this information to the schools that you listed in the FAFSA.

Note: *It is a good idea to apply for financial aid prior to the semester that you plan to attend school, as it could take several weeks, sometimes months, to determine your financial aid award. Contact your school's financial aid department to inquire about processing time.*

Financial Aid Award (Budget)

The financial aid departments at each school will then determine a loan and/or grant amount, calculated in part by the cost of tuition and other expenses for that particular school, and will notify you of your award, either electronically or by mail. Your award will indicate the amount of money that the school is willing to loan or grant you to attend their facility. The award will also usually indicate and itemize the expenses for attending the school and living expenses, including gas to and from school, cost of books, food, and other expenses. These expenses add up to your financial budget.

The dollar amount indicated in your award is generally for annual tuition, meaning for a full year. If your enrollment status changes and you attend a different amount of classes than what you indicated when filling out the FAFSA, your award amount will automatically change, depending on your enrollment status.

Once you receive your award you are cleared to enroll in classes, depending on the school. In most instances the school will allow you to enroll in classes without having to pay any tuition fees up front before receiving your financial aid. Once you enroll the cost of tuition will be automatically deducted from your award balance for that semester and the school will refund the difference to you.

Financial Aid Refund

Once you have enrolled in classes, the school will deduct the cost of tuition from your financial aid award (budget) and the remaining dollar amount will be refunded to you. For example, if the cost of attending school full-time is $1,200 per quarter and the school awards you $18,000 per year, divide the yearly amount by the number of quarters the school has per year. Then subtract the cost of tuition from that amount. The difference will be the amount of your refund.

In this example we'll use a 4 quarter system, making the award per quarter $4,500 ($18,000 per year ÷ 4 quarters = $4,500 per quarter). Then subtract the cost of tuition from the award per quarter ($4,500 per quarter – $1,200 tuition per quarter = $3,300 refund per quarter). You would receive a refund from the school in the amount of $3,300 each quarter that you attend. You, the student, can do whatever you want with this money, whether it is buy a new car, put it in the bank, or something else, although this money is intended to be used for education related expenses and to achieve your educational goals.

Direct Deposit

You can also fill out a direct deposit form at the school's financial aid office and the money will be automatically deposited into your bank account. This is recommended as it is usually much quicker and the money will be deposited before most students who don't apply for direct deposit receive theirs.

Emerging Technology

With the emergence of new technology many schools are now going paperless and instead are dispersing funds electronically using debit cards. Also, notifications of deposited funds can be sent to your smart phone immediately notifying you of disbursement.

Some schools provide an online portal, or website, that you can access to check your financial aid status and related information. This portal allows you to see which documents are being requested by the financial aid department, which documents have been submitted, your enrollment status, and view your award. It also provides downloadable forms that might be needed and gives disbursement dates in case you are wondering when you will receive your aid.

Disbursement Dates

Each school has financial aid disbursement dates. In the past schools would disburse your entire award all in one disbursement. Because many students drop out of school before completing their classes, some schools have now divided up your financial aid award to be disbursed over several different dates throughout the semester. For example, a school might disburse one third of your aid on three different dates spread throughout the semester. For example, if your award for a Fall semester is $1,200, you might get $400 on September 14, $400 on November 1, and $400 on December 14. This is done to protect schools from disbursing aid to students who don't complete their classes.

Steps to Applying for Financial Aid

Step 1 ☐ Fill out a FAFSA online indicating the schools you are considering attending. This can be done online by visiting fafsa.gov.

Step 2 ☐ Apply for admission to a school and be accepted to the school.

Step 3 ☐ Apply to a degree program and be accepted into that program.

- There are usually no requirements to take general education classes at the junior or community college levels, other than basic reading, writing, and math requirements. However, some colleges might require you to choose a major in order to receive aid.
- Each degree or major will have its own requirements. Some of these requirements include GPA (Grade Point Average), prior degrees or educational tract, prerequisite classes, preparatory tests scores, such as the GRE (Graduate Record Examination) or GMAT (Graduate Management Admission Test), to name a couple, as well as letters of recommendation from prior instructors or employers.

Step 4 ☐ Enroll in classes (at least half-time for student loans) and maintain enrollment for the duration of the semester. (VVC flyer, n.d.)

Note: *You don't necessarily have to be accepted into a major to enroll in classes. Step 3 applies generally to advanced programs, such as Bachelor's, Master's, and Doctorate degree programs.*

Chapter 2

Attending College

Types of Schools

Kindergarten through High School

Kindergarten, elementary, junior high (middle school), and high school provide basic education before starting college.

Junior and Community Colleges

These types of colleges are usually located according to neighborhoods or communities. Students can earn Associate degrees and Certifications at these types of colleges. This is where most students begin college, taking general education classes and deciding on a major. Completing general education at this level is usually a prerequisite before proceeding to a university, however, students may elect, if they choose, to take their general education at the university level as well. Junior and Community College facilities are usually much smaller than universities.

Universities

Universities offer Bachelor's, Master's degrees, and Doctorate degrees, which entail a more in-depth learning experience. They have larger budgets than community colleges and offer more professional equipment and facilities, such as labs and recording studios, for hands-on experience. These schools are primarily government funded.

There are two public university systems, which vary by state.

- State University System (i.e. California State University)
- University State System (i.e. University of California)

Private Schools

Some private schools are also known as universities or are comparable to the university level. They are usually more expensive to attend, harder to get into, and known for their astute reputation.

Professional Schools

Examples of professional schools are medical schools and law schools, to name a couple. Admittance to these schools usually requires you to hold a bachelor's degree in the particular field of study for which you will attend.

Medical Schools

Medical schools can provide degrees related to the medical field, such as Psychiatry, which is an M.D. (Medical Doctor), and other medical titles, such as D.O. (Orthodontist), Dentist (D.D.S.), Chiropractor (DC), Ophthalmologist (OPHTH), Neurologist, etc. These are but a few of many specialized branches of the medical and dental degrees.

Law Schools

Law schools provide legal degrees, such as the JD (Juris Doctorate). Those with JDs become lawyers and attorneys. Lawyers can also be prosecutors (district attorneys) and public defenders, and later can become judges. Another degree offered by law schools is the Legal Document Assistant (LDA). LDAs become paralegals.

Levels of Education (In Order)

Diploma

A diploma is a degree of education earned when graduating from high school. This consists of basic education completed from kindergarten through 12th grade. A GED (General Education Development) is equivalent to obtaining a high school diploma.

Associate Degree

During this level of education, the main focus is on general education, such as math, English, and writing, although some classes may focus on a degree objective. This level of degree is usually earned at a junior or community college.

- This degree typically takes 2 years to complete on average.

Baccalaureate (Bachelor's Degree)

This level of education focuses on completing a major and minor degree objective.

- At this level of education, a student is considered to be an Undergraduate student.
- This degree typically takes 4 years to complete on average.

Master's Degree

This level of education focuses on advanced classes usually related to your major, but can be unrelated.

- At this level of education, a student is considered to be a Graduate student.
- This degree typically takes 2 to 4 years to complete on average.

Doctorate Degree

This level of education focuses on even more advanced classes usually specializing in a profession. Students at this stage are sometimes referred to as scholars and earn degrees such as a PhD (Doctor of Philosophy), an M.D. (Medical Doctor), or a JD (Juris Doctorate – law degree), to name a few.

- At this level of education, a student is considered to be a Post Graduate student.
- This is considered to be the highest level of education.
- This degree typically takes 2 to 4 years to complete on average.

Note: *A Master's in Fine Arts (MFA) is considered by some to be the "creative equivalent" of a "research doctorate" or professional degree.*

Degree Elements

Major

A major is a degree objective that is considered to be your main course of academic study. This usually requires more classes to complete than a minor and is the main focus of a student's academic career.

Minor

A minor is a degree objective that is considered to be secondary to your major. This usually requires fewer classes to complete. The purpose of choosing a minor is to expand or broaden a student's area of study, which usually broadens a student's employment opportunity. Sometimes a minor is also chosen to compliment or strengthen the major area of study. For example, a Business major might have a minor in Accounting. However, a minor may be in a completely different topic unrelated to the major.

Internship

Prior to completing your degree, you may have to fulfill an internship requirement, depending on the degree. An internship is when a student is employed at an organization or company that contracts with the school to get hands-on experience. Most internships are performed with little or no monetary compensation. The idea is that you gain real life experience in your field of study in exchange for your service. It is a good way to build relationships with others in the field and expose yourself to opportunities. Internships can also lead to jobs with the companies that offer them.

Program Requirements

Each degree or major program will have its own requirements. Some of these requirements include GPA (Grade Point Average), prior degrees or educational tract, prerequisite classes, performance tests scores, such as the

GRE (Graduate Record Examination) or GMAT (Graduate Management Admission Test), to name a couple, as well as letters of recommendation from prior instructors or employers.

Grade Point Average (GPA)

Having a certain GPA may be a requirement to enter certain colleges or degree programs. A student's grade point average (GPA) is a score calculated by dividing the total number of grade points earned by the total number of credit hours, or units, attempted. Your GPA can range from 0.0 to 4.0. Grade points are associated with a letter grade (A=4, B=3, C=2, D=1, F=0).

For example, if you enroll in 3 classes (a 4-unit class, a 3-unit class, and a 2-unit class), and you receive an A, a B, and a D, you would calculate your GPA as follows: The total number of grade points earned is 27, [(letter grade A(4) x 4 units = 16) + (letter grade B(3) x 3 units = 9) + (letter grade D(1) x 2 units = 2)]. The total number of grade points earned is 27, (16 + 9 + 2). Now, divide the total number of grade points earned (27) by the total number of credit hours, or units, attempted (9), (4 units + 3 units + 2 units = 9 units), and (27 ÷ 9) = 3.00. Your GPA would be 3.00.

Prerequisites

Prerequisites are classes that are required to be completed before you can take another class or enter a degree program.

Transcripts

Transcripts are a record of classes that you've taken at other schools. These can help to reduce the number of classes you will have to take to complete a major. For example, a Communications Law class that you have previously taken at another school may apply to a Communications major that you are attempting to complete at the school you are applying to, and therefore eliminate the need to take that class again. There is usually a small fee associated with obtaining transcripts.

Preparatory and Degree Program Admission Tests

A preparatory test, or prep test, is a test designed to show your aptitude at a certain educational level or in a specific educational area. These tests may be required to enter some degree programs or schools. For example, to enter the MBA (Masters of Business Administration) program you may be required to take the GMAT (Graduate Management Admission Test), or to enter the MA in Education program you may be required to take the GRE (Graduate Record Examination), to name a couple. You would take the LSAT (Law School Admission Test) if you were trying to get into law school (National…, 2025).

There are many types of these tests. They usually have a fee associated with them and have to be taken at a testing facility where you are timed and recorded on video camera. Some can be taken online. These tests can last as long as 4 hours. How well you do on them may determine whether you are admitted into a degree program or not. There are study guides for each of these tests available for you to practice with at most libraries and bookstores. The financial aid office can offer you a voucher to pay for the cost of the test once in a year period.

Preparatory tests are taken to get into a school, degree program, to obtain a scholarship, or simply identify your strengths & weaknesses. There are many 'prep' tests available. Below are a few of the more common ones:

- SAT (Scholarship Assessment Test)
- PSAT (Preliminary Scholarship Assessment Test)
- ACT (American College Test)
- LSAT (Law School Admission Test)
- MCAT (Medical College Admission Test)
- MSAT (Medical School Admission Test)
- ISEE (Independent School Entrance Exam)
- GED (General Education Development)
- TOEFL (Test Of English as a Foreign Language)

- GMAT (Graduate Management Admission Test)
- GRE (Graduate Record Examination)
- DAT (Dental Admission Test)
- OAT (Optometry Admission Test)
- ASVAB (Armed Services Vocational Aptitude Battery)

Services Offered by the School

Going to school can be a cumbersome undertaking when you are getting started, but don't let that sway you from trying. The school has an abundance of resources to answer your every need and help you succeed, including resources for disabled and international students.

Admissions Counselors

If you feel lost and have lots of questions that need answers it is a good idea to make an appointment with an admissions counselor. He or she can answer questions regarding enrolling in school successfully.

Career Counselors

Career counselors help you decide what you want to do with your life and explore career options. They give you an idea of how much money different occupations make and help you decide on a major. Sometimes they give you aptitude and interest tests, which tell you what your strengths and weaknesses are in different areas of study. For example, after taking an occupational interest test you may realize that you excel in electronics and are not so great at music. Based on these results you can decide what major you wish to pursue.

Major Acceptance Offices

Each major will have a main office that handles the affairs of that major, such as the Office of Education, the Office of Computer Science, or the

MBA (Masters of Business Administration) Office, to name a few. These offices will have counselors to help you do the necessary paperwork to apply for their program. Each of these offices will have their own applications for admission and their own requirements for getting into that program. You may have to provide GRE and GMAT test scores, or the equivalent, for these programs as well.

Services for Students with Disabilities Offices

Each school has an office that offers services to students with disabilities. For more information about services for students with disabilities, see Chapter 3.

International Students Offices

These offices help students from foreign countries succeed in enrollment and other career counseling areas, as well as transitioning from a foreign school or culture. This office can also help you find housing and employment as well.

Campus Housing Office

If available, schools that offer housing will have a housing office that handles the affairs of students living on campus or at nearby housing areas. This office can answer questions about the cost of living in campus housing, as well as what amenities and features are offered.

Medical Center

Each school usually has a medical facility available to students. At these facilities you can have all kinds of medical tests done. You can be evaluated by real doctors, who can prescribe medications, and perform tests on you if needed. The cost of this is partly included in your school tuition. There may be a small fee to have certain medical tests or procedures performed.

Counseling Center

Some schools offer counseling services. These services include psychological counseling for various needs, such as: coping with stress, interpersonal relationships, family and life counseling, personality disorders, and goal orientation, to name a few.

Ombudsman

The school ombudsman is a mediary there to help you resolve problems with school employees. For example, if you feel you are being treated unfairly by an instructor, the ombudsman will act as a middleman to help investigate and resolve the problem.

Student Affairs

The student affairs office is there to help students in a variety of ways, from resolving problems with employees to getting help finding housing and a broad range of other services. If you don't know where to begin finding an answer to a question, the student affairs office is the place to go.

Student ID

Once you have been admitted to a school, you will be assigned a Student Identification Number (SID) and will receive a Student ID Card from the school. You will need this throughout your academic career to have access to many services that the school has to offer.

Student Union

The Student Union offers lots of services to students, including legal services, job placement, and many other services. Tickets for movies, theme parks, special events, and various entertainment activities can be purchased here at discounted prices.

Career Center

Sometimes referred to as the Job Placement Center, this office can help you with finding a job. They offer services, such as: creating a resume, mock interviews, career advice, and have job postings from various employers.

Library

The school library has many services available aside from the standard checking out of media. School library systems are linked to one another throughout the country. Each of these systems has a different name, for example the Link+ system. If you are unable to find a needed book in the library or can't afford to buy a text book, you can search the linked systems to borrow these books from other colleges or public libraries and never pay for them. Keep in mind the due dates indicated upon checkout to avoid late fees.

Transcripts Office

The Transcripts office helps students obtain transcripts from other schools. You will have to fill out a transcript request form and pay a small fee when requesting them. This office will send the request to any schools you listed on the form as having attended to obtain records from those schools. If you obtain transcripts from previous schools yourself, the envelope they come in must be sealed and stamped by the college. Otherwise, they will not be accepted.

Requirements to Attend School

Diploma and GED Requirements

Usually the school will require that you show proof of having graduated from high school with a diploma or having a GED (General Education Diploma), which is the equivalent of a high school diploma. The GED is usually obtained through adult school classes by those who never graduated from high school. However, don't be dismayed if you don't have either of these.

Entrance Exams

After applying to and being admitted to a school, the school will administer an entrance exam. Everyone who intends on attending the school must take this exam. The entrance exam will test your ability to read, write, and perform basic math skills. If you fail to pass the writing requirement, you will have to take a writing class to boost your skills. Satisfying the writing requirement is also necessary when applying to higher level degree and major programs.

Rationale for Tests and Requirements

The purpose of requiring a high school diploma or GED and taking the entrance exam is to determine that you have the ability to perform the basic skills required to succeed in school. The school doesn't want to place you in a position in which you will likely fail due to a lack of ability to perform adequately. This is the main purpose of the entrance requirements. Therefore, by requiring proof that you have general education skills, the school is assured that you are ready to begin college.

Entrance exams tell the school what skill level of classes to start you in. For example, the school might offer ESL (English as a Second Language) classes to help those who don't read or write the English language very well to develop necessary basic reading and writing skills.

What to Do if You Don't Meet the Entrance Criteria

Some schools may admit you on a conditional basis or will offer (some free) classes to help students succeed in meeting the entrance criteria. The school may allow you to enroll in ESL classes, which are beginner classes. However, the school may also refer you to an adult school to develop adequate general education skills. Each school is different so you will have to check with each one to see what their requirements are. Some schools may let you attend regardless of your prior education.

Steps to Enroll in College

Step 1 ☐ Apply for admission to the school. Obtain an application for admission to the school of your choice. Most schools have online applications. Complete the application for approval. There may be a fee associated with the application for admission. Sometimes you can apply for a fee waiver to avoid paying the admission fee. Once accepted you will be assigned a Student Identification Number (SID) and can receive a Student ID Card from the school. You will need this throughout your academic career. Once you have applied to the school and been accepted, you will need to choose a degree objective, such as a major or minor area of study. The classes you choose to take will be determined by your degree objective.

Step 2 ☐ Obtain a class schedule and choose which classes you wish to take. Most schools now offer online class schedules and registration.

Step 3 ☐ Register (enroll in classes.) This can be done either in person at the school, online, or over the phone. The quickest and easiest way is to enroll over the phone or online to avoid standing in long lines.

Step 4 ☐ Attend classes. Once you have enrolled, it is important that you attend the first and second classes to ensure yourself a seat. Some instructors may drop you from the class if you do not show up in order to give students who want or need to be in the classes a seat. Likewise, if you were unable to enroll in a class that you wish to take because it was full, you can go to the class anyway during the first or second meeting and ask the instructor to let you join the class. You may be able due to other students not attending or who have dropped the class.

Congratulations! You are now enrolled and attending school.

Note: *Depending on your educational level you may need to obtain transcripts from prior schools you've attended in order to be admitted to the school you plan on attending.*

Chapter 3

Services for Students with Disabilities

Services for Students with Disabilities

There is a wealth of services available to ensure equal opportunities to students with verified temporary or permanent disabilities. Qualifying disabilities include: blind or other visual impairments, communication impairments, deaf and hard of hearing, learning disabilities, mobility disabilities, psychiatric disabilities, and other functional disabilities.

Services available for students with disabilities include the following academic support services, adaptive equipment, and work-related services.

Academic Support Services

- Priority registration
- Mobility assistance
- In class and library assistance
- Sign language interpreters
- Note taking services
- Real time captioning
- Approved course related printed materials in brail
- Alternate media including textbooks and course materials in electronic, audio, enlarged, and MP3 format

Adaptive Equipment

- Dragon Dictation software
- Assistive listening devices
- Closed caption decoding
- CCTV reader
- 4-track tape recorders

- JAWS screen reading software
- ZoomText screen magnification software
- Large-screen monitors

Students with temporary disabilities, such as from an accident, illness, injury, or surgery, can receive services on a provisional basis.

Work-Related Services for Students with Disabilities

Workability IV (WAIV)

Workability IV is a program offered in cooperation between your school and the Department of Rehabilitation (DOR). You must be a client of the DOR and currently attending school or planning to transfer in order to participate in this program. (Services..., 2011)

WAIV offers the following services for <u>prospective</u> students:

- Assessments for school eligibility
- Guidance through admissions and financial aid
- Assistance with course selection and enrollment

WAIV offers the following services for <u>enrolled</u> students:

- Creation of an educational plan for the DOR
- Access to campus services (disability services, assistive computer technology, tutoring, adult re-entry)
- An on-campus resource to answer questions

WAIV is comprised of two components: Employment Services 1 (ES1) and Employment Services 2 (ES2) and offer the following services:

ES1

- Resume creation
- Assistance with obtaining internships, part time jobs, and volunteer positions
- Monthly WAIV to Work trainings
- Career center orientation
- Interview preparation for Federal internship recruitment programs
- Mock interviews
- Career and transferable skills assessment workshops

ES2

- Job Application Assistance
- Job Placement
- One-on-one job search coaching
- Cover letter creation
- Critique of interview skills
- Resume refining and updating

Chapter 4

Military and Veterans Financial Aid

Military and Veterans Financial Aid

Post 9/11-G.I. Bill

The Post 9/11-G.I. Bill is available for those who wish to pursue approved graduate and undergraduate degrees, vocational/technical training, on-the-job training, flight training, correspondence training, entrepreneurship training, licensing and national testing programs, and tutorial assistance. It offers financial support to cover housing and educational expenses to those in the military who have completed 90 days of aggregate service after September 11, 2011, or who were discharged due to a service related disability after 30 days. The discharge cannot have been negative in nature.

The Post 9/11-G.I. Bill includes the following:

- Full tuition and fees for students attending a public school in-state. For students attending private or foreign schools, tuition and fees have a cap of $17,500 per academic year.
- You may be eligible for a higher reimbursement rate if you are attending a private school in AZ, MI, NH, NY, PA, SC or TX. Also, the "Yellow Ribbon Program" (see below) is available and can help to reimburse the difference of tuition if you are attending a more expensive public or private school as a non-resident out-of-state student.
- A monthly housing allowance, called MHA.
- A stipend of $1,000 for books and supplies, paid annually based on enrollment.
- A one-time rural benefit payment is available for eligible individuals.
- Benefits may be transferred to dependents for some members.

Note: *For purposes of the FAFSA, veterans are considered to be independent and do not need to report their parents' income.*

The Montgomery G.I. Bill (MGIB)

There are two types of the MGIB:

- MGIB-AD (Chapter 30) is for active duty personnel. Members pay $100 a month for 12 months, and after completion of a minimum service obligation can receive a monthly education benefit.

- MGIB-SR (Chapter 1606) is for reservists who are active in drilling and have a 6-year service obligation in the selected reserve.

Under the MGIB benefits are usually paid within 2 weeks after enrollment has been verified at the end of each month of completed school.

The Yellow Ribbon Program

Under this program participating Institutions of Higher Learning contribute additional funds to those who receive the Post 9/11-G.I. Bill, which are matched by the VA (Veterans Administration), and made available for your education program. Yellow Ribbon benefits are available for a limited number of individuals as stated in their participation agreement. Only veterans are eligible for this program. Active duty and their spouses are not. Participating schools must certify your enrollment to the VA. In order to qualify for this program:

- You must be eligible to receive the maximum benefit rate under the Post-9/11 G.I. Bill.

- You must have served an aggregate period of at least 36 months of active duty after September 10, 2001.

- You must have been discharged honorably from active duty service due to a service related disability; and have served 30 continuous days after September 10, 2001.

- You must be a dependent who is eligible for Transfer of Entitlement under the Post-9/11 G.I. Bill based on the veteran's service criteria mentioned above.

- Your school must participate in the Yellow Ribbon Program.

Veterans Educational Assistance Program (VEAP)

VEAP is an educational benefit program that is available to you if you made contributions from your military pay to participate in the program. Your contributions are matched $2 for every $1 by the U.S. Government. You are entitled to receive these benefits from 1 to 36 months depending on your number of monthly contributions, and they must be used within 10 years of your release from active duty service. Any entitled funds unused at the end of the 10-year period will be refunded to you. To be eligible to receive VEAP benefits:

- You must have begun service for the first time between January 1, 1977, and June 30, 1985.
- You must have opened a contribution account before April 1, 1987.
- You must have contributed an amount of $25 to $2700.
- You must have completed your first required period of service.
- You must have been had a discharge that was not considered dishonorable.

The National Call to Service Incentive Program (NCS)

This program is offered by the Department of Defense, but administered by the VA. Participants must complete a period of service to be eligible and can choose from incentives, such as:

- A cash bonus of $5,000.
- Repayment up to $18,000 of a qualifying student loan.
- Entitlement to an allowance equal to the 3-year monthly Chapter 30 rate for 1 year.
- Entitlement to an allowance equal to 50% of the less-than-3-year monthly Chapter 30 rate for 3 years.
- Payment of amounts you are eligible for of Chapter 1606 or

Chapter 30 benefits minus any amounts paid by the NCS program.

In order to receive benefits under the NCS program you must meet all of the following requirements:

- First, you must complete 15 months of active duty service in a military occupation specialty designated by the Secretary of Defense.
- Second, without a break in service you must then serve an additional 2 years on active duty status in the selected reserve, or a period of duty determined by the Secretary of Defense.
- Third, after you have completed this portion of service without break, the remaining service for which you are obligated to complete will be served as follows:
    - In the armed forces on active duty
    - In the selected reserve
    - In the Individual Ready Reserve
    - In AmeriCorps, or a domestic national service jointly designated by the Secretary of Defense.

The Veterans Retraining Assistance Program

This program was created as part of the VOW to Hire Heroes Act of 2011 in order to retrain veterans that have been significantly affected by current economic conditions. It offers 1 year of training to unemployed veterans. In order to qualify, a veteran must:

- Be between the ages of 35 and 60.
- Be unemployed.
- Be honorably discharged.
- Be enrolled in a VA approved education program offered at a community college or technical school that leads to an Associate

degree, Non-College degree, or a Certification, and trains the veteran for an occupation in high demand.

- Not be eligible for any other VA education benefit program.
- Not be receiving VA compensation due to employability.
- Not be enrolled in a state or federal job training program.

Survivors and Dependents Educational Assistance Program

Under this program, members can receive up to 45 months of education and training opportunities. To qualify for this program:

- You must be a son, daughter, or spouse of a person who died as related to being in the service, is MIA (missing in action), or is captured in the line of duty and forcibly detained in a foreign country.
- Sons and daughters must be between 18 and 26 years of age.
- Spousal benefits end 10 years after eligibility starts or when the veteran dies.

Other Military Educational Benefit Programs

Each branch of the armed services has some form of scholarship available for education. For example, the Army, Marines, Navy, Air Force, and Coast Guard all have scholarships available that service members can apply for. To find out about these, contact your service of interest.

Veterans On-Line Application (VONAPP)

The VONAPP is an online application that veterans can use to apply for various benefits, including educational benefits. (VA.gov, 2025)

Chapter 5

International Students Financial Aid

International Students Financial Aid

International Students

International students can be U.S. citizens, who plan on attending international schools in foreign countries, and foreign students, who plan on attending schools in the U.S. Financial aid is available for both and is offered by the U.S. federal government and by private organizations or lending institutions.

Requirements for Receiving International Student Loans

In order to receive U.S. federal (Type IV) financial aid you must be either a U.S. citizen or eligible non-citizen, and have earned a high school diploma or equivalent, such as a General Education Development Certificate (GED). If you have not met this requirement you will have to demonstrate that you have the ability to benefit, which can be done by passing an approved ability-to-benefit test (ATB).

U.S. federal loans for international students require a U.S. co-signer. This means that a credit-worthy U.S. citizen or permanent resident (an eligible non-citizen) must co-sign for the loan.

Eligible Non-citizen

An eligible non-citizen is anyone who is not a U.S. citizen, but is any of the following:

- a U.S. national (a native of American Samoa or Swain's Island)
- a U.S. permanent resident that holds a Permanent Resident Card, such as an I-151, I-551, or I-551C
- a citizen of the Republic of Palau (PW), a citizen of the Republic of the Marshall Islands (MH), or a citizen of the Federated States of Micronesia (FM)
- an eligible non-citizen that has an Arrival-Departure Record (I-94) from the Department of Homeland Security or U.S. Citizenship

and Immigration Services (USCIS) that shows one of the following as a designation:

- "Refugee"
- "Asylum Granted"
- "Cuban-Haitian Entrant, Status Pending"
- "Conditional Entrant" (only valid if issued before April 1, 1980)
- a victim of human trafficking, a T-visa holder (T-2, T-3, T-4, etc.)
- "Parolee", you must be paroled in the U.S. for at least one year and provide evidence from the USCIS that you are in the U.S. for other than a temporary purpose and have the intention of becoming a U.S. citizen or permanent resident.

You are not eligible for federal student aid if you:

- only have a Notice of Approval for Permanent Residence (I-171 or I-464)
- are in the U.S. and hold an F1 or F2 student visa
- are in the U.S. and hold a J1 or J2 exchange visitor visa
- hold a G series visa (pertaining to international organizations)

Eligible Program

In order to receive federal aid, you must be enrolled in an eligible program. An eligible program is a program of organized instruction or study that will lead to an academic, professional, or vocational degree or certificate, or other recognized educational credential. There are 2 exceptions:

1. You can get a Stafford loan for up to 1 year to complete preparatory

coursework for a program that a school has said that you must take in order to qualify for admission into its program.

2. You can get a Federal Work-Study, Federal Perkins Loan, a Stafford Loan, or your parents can get a PLUS loan if you're in enrolled at least half-time in a program to obtain a professional credential or certification required by a state for employment as an elementary or secondary school teacher.

US Students Attending School Internationally

The following section will discuss financial aid available to US students who plan on studying internationally, whether in a study abroad program while attending a US school, or enrolling in a foreign school.

Study Abroad Loans

If you are a US undergraduate or graduate student enrolled in an approved school in the United States, you can apply for a loan to cover the cost of a study abroad program if you are planning to study abroad for a few semesters. It is not necessary to complete a FAFSA to receive study abroad loans. However, you must meet the following criteria:

- You must receive credit for the study abroad program in the college or university you are attending in the US.
- You must be a US citizen or permanent resident.
- You must have a co-signer. The co-signer must be a US citizen or permanent resident with good credit and income history that has lived in the US for the past 2 years.

Other benefits of study abroad loans include:

- You can borrow up to the total cost of attendance, minus other aid
- Flexible repayment terms are available
- There are thousands of approved schools

Foreign Enrolled Loans

If you are a US student planning on enrolling in a foreign school, funding options are more limited. The cost of attending foreign schools is typically more expensive than attending US schools. You will most likely have to take out an international student loan, as federal funding, upon completion of a FAFSA, will most likely not cover the remaining tuition cost. A co-signer is not required; however, it is recommended. Co-signers must be a US citizen or permanent resident with good credit and income history that has lived in the US for the past 2 years.

Foreign enrolled loans have the following benefits:

- The total cost of education, which typically includes tuition, room and board, and living expenses, minus other aid received can be borrowed
- Application and approval can be done quickly online
- There are no out-of-pocket costs or application fees
- There are hundreds of approved foreign schools, including professional schools, such as dental, medical, business, and law schools

International Students Attending School in the US

The following section will discuss financial aid available to international students who plan on attending a school in the US.

International Student Loans

If you are an international student planning on attending a school in the United States, you can apply for an international student loan from private lenders in the US. A co-signer is required and all co-signers must be a US citizen or permanent resident with good credit and income history that has lived in the US for the past 2 years. (Dedicated...,2011)

International student loans offer the following benefits:

- They have flexible repayment terms
- There is no collateral required
- Application can be made online

Some things to know about international student loans are:

- A US co-signer is required from a US citizen or permanent resident with good credit and income history that has lived in the US for the past 2 years
- Repayment can be deferred while you are in school and for up to six months after you finish school. Also, repayment terms can extend up to 20 years and can be paid off early without penalty
- The total cost of education, which typically includes tuition, room and board, and living expenses, minus other aid received can be borrowed. Some programs offer $30,000 or even up to $50,000 or more per year
- Interest rates are variable, which means that your rate and payment amount will move up and down with the LIBOR index.

The LIBOR (London Interbank Offered Rate) is the primary index benchmark, which is the average interest rate estimated by leading London banks.

International Student Loan Lenders

The following is a list some US banks that offer loans to international students. Most of them, if not all, will require a US co-signer who is a US citizen or permanent resident with good credit and income history that has lived in the US for the past 2 years. Some may have restrictions on the type of visa you hold:

- Canadian Higher Education Loan Program (CanHELP)
- Credila Financial Services

- Global Student Loan Corporation (GSLC)
- International Student Loan Program (ISLP)
- Study Abroad Loan Program (SALP)
- Massachusetts Educational Financing Authority (MEFA)
- Norwest Bank
- The Education Resources Institute (TERI)

NAFSA: Association of International Educators

NAFSA is a non-profit professional organization dedicated to promoting international education and making international public policies known worldwide to bridge the gap between nations. Its primary role is to connect educators, students, scholars, and foreign citizens in order to establish mutual understanding among nations, prepare future generations with cross-cultural skills, and help create conditions for a more peaceful world. The NAFSA website link is nafsa.org. (NAFSA.org, 2011)

eduPASS

eduPASS is an Internet site that provides information to international students who are considering pursuing undergraduate, graduate, or professional education in the United States. This site also contains information for international students who are already in the US, as well as information for students considering study in other countries. The site provides information on admissions, financing, scholarships, visas, and ESL (English as a Second Language). The website link is edpuass.org.

Appendices

Appendix A

Annual Loan Limits

Dependent Students

Annual Loan Limits - Stafford Loan			
Dependent Students (except whose parents were unable to obtain a PLUS loan)	**Combined Base Limit for Subsidized and Unsubsidized Loans**	**Additional Limit for Unsubsidized Loans**	**Total Limit for Unsubsidized Loans** (minus subsidized amounts)
First-Year Undergraduate (Freshman)	$3,500	$2,000	$5,500
Second-Year Undergraduate (Sophomore)	$4,500	$2,000	$6,500
Third-Year and Beyond Undergraduate (Junior, Senior)	$5,500	$2,000	$7,500
Preparatory Coursework (for enrollment in an undergraduate program)	$2,625	$0	$2,625

Preparatory Coursework (for enrollment in a graduate or professional program)	$5,500	$0	$5,500
Teacher Certification Coursework	$5,500	$0	$5,500

Independent Students

Independent Students (and dependent students whose parents were denied a PLUS loan)	**Combined Base Limit for Subsidized and Unsubsidized Loans**	**Additional Limit for Unsubsidized Loans**	**Total Limit for Unsubsidized Loans** (minus subsidized amounts)
First-Year Undergraduate (Freshman)	$3,500	$6,000	$9,500
Second-Year Undergraduate (Sophomore)	$4,500	$6,000	$10,500
Third-Year and Beyond Undergraduate (Junior, Senior)	$5,500	$7,000	$12,500
Preparatory Coursework (for enrollment in an undergraduate program)	$2,625	$6,000	$8,625
Preparatory Coursework (for enrollment in a graduate or professional program)	$5,500	$7,000	$12,500
Teacher Certification Coursework	$5,500	$7,000	$12,500

Appendix A

Graduate and Professional Students

Graduate and Professional Students	**Combined Base Limit for Subsidized and Unsubsidized Loans**	**Additional Limit for Unsubsidized Loans**	**Total Limit for Unsubsidized Loans** (minus subsidized amounts)
Graduate and Professional Students	$8,500	$12,000	$20,500
Medical School Students	$8,500	$32,000	$40,500

(studentaid.gov, 2025)

Appendix B

Aggregate Loan Limits

Aggregate Loan Limits - Stafford Loan			
	Combined Base Limit for Subsidized and Unsubsidized Loans	**Additional Limit for Unsubsidized Loans**	**Total Limit for Unsubsidized Loans** (minus subsidized amounts)
Dependent Undergraduate Students (whose parents were not denied a PLUS loan)	$23,000	$8,000	$31,000
Independent Undergraduate Students (and dependent students whose parents were denied a PLUS loan)	$23,000	$34,500	$57,500
Graduate and Professional Students	$65,500 (including undergraduate Stafford loans)	$73,000	$138,500
Medical School Students (Effective 4/18/08)	$65,500 (including undergraduate Stafford loans)	$158,500	$224,000

(studentaid.gov, 2025)

Appendix C

Pell Grant Limits

Pell Grant Limits (based on Full-time status)		
Year	**Minimum Pell Grant**	**Maximum Pell Grant**
2020-21	$486	$6,395
2021-22	$555	$6,495
2022-23	$692	$6,895
2023-24	$750	$7,395
2024-25	$740	$7,395
2025-26	$740	$7,395

(studentaid.gov, 2025)

Appendix D

Loan Interest Rates

Interest Rates on Subsidized Stafford Loans for Undergraduate Students & Unsubsidized Stafford Loans / Graduate Stafford Loans		
Year	**Interest Rate Subsidized Stafford Loans** (Undergraduate Students)	**Interest Rate Unsubsidized & Graduate Stafford Loans** (Unsubsidized / Graduate)
2019-20	4.53%	4.53% / 6.08%
2020-21	2.75%	2.75% / 4.30%
2021-22	3.73%	3.73% / 5.28%
2022-23	4.99%	4.99% / 6.54%
2023-24	5.50%	5.50% / 7.05%
2024-25	6.53%	6.53% / 8.08%
2025-26	6.53%* *subject to change	6.53%* / 8.08%* *subject to change

(studentaid.gov, 2025)

Glossary

academic	of, relating to, or characteristic of a school, especially one of higher learning.
academic probation	a trial period in which a student is given time to try to redeem failing grades or bad conduct.
accrued	to increase, accumulate, or come about as a result of growth.
ACT	American College Test. Measures high school students' general educational development and their capability to complete college level work with the multiple choice tests covering four skill areas: English, mathematics, reading, and science.
admission	the state or privilege of being admitted, or being allowed to attend.
adverse	unfavorable; opposed to one's interests.
aggregate	the accumulated total, or whole sum or amount.
annual	occurring or happening every year or once a year.
APLE program	a teacher incentive program designed to place students, interns, and teachers in low income areas, after which a portion of their loans can be forgiven.
application	a form used to request admittance to a college or program.
aptitude	capacity for learning.
Associate degree	a degree conferred especially by a community or junior college.
association	an organization of persons having a common interest.
ASVAB	Armed Services Vocational Aptitude Battery. A multiple choice test, administered by the United States Military Entrance Processing Command, used to determine qualification for enlistment in the United States armed forces.

attend	to be present at.
award	something that is conferred or bestowed especially on the basis of merit or need.
Bachelor's degree	an academic degree conferred on someone who has successfully completed undergraduate studies.
balance	the difference between an amount due and an amount paid.
bank	a financial establishment that invests money deposited by customers, pays it out when required, makes loans at interest, and exchanges currency.
bill	a printed or written statement of charges indicating an amount of money owed for goods supplied or services rendered.
binding	involving an obligation that cannot be broken.
borrow	take and use (money) from a person or bank under an agreement to pay it back later.
budget	the amount of money needed or available for a purpose.
campus	the grounds and buildings of a university or college.
cancellation	the annulling of a legal document.
capitalize	to record and carry forward into one or more future periods any expenditure the benefits or process from which will then be realized.
career	working permanently in or committed to a particular profession.
catalog	a list of courses offered by a university or college.
cease	bring (a specified action) to an end.
certification	a designation earned by a person to assure qualification to perform a job or task.

check	a written order to a bank to pay a stated sum from the drawer's account.
class schedule	a list of classes offered during a semester and times during which they meet.
college	an educational institution or establishment.
community college	a nonresidential junior college offering courses to people living in a particular area.
compensation	payment in the form or money or other received by person in exchange for their services.
consolidate	to combine several financial accounts into a single account.
cost	the amount of money required to be paid for something.
credit report	a report consisting of a record of creditor accounts indicating their status.
credit union	a financial institution owned by its members that provides loans and other services to its members.
criteria	a set of requirements.
cumulative	Increasing or enlarging by successive addition.
DAT	Dental Admission Test. A multiple choice standardized exam taken by potential dental school students.
decal	a card or sticker, usually placed on an automobile, to indicate the right to park.
default	to be in violation of the terms of agreement of repaying, or failure to pay on, a loan.
deferment	the state of postponing payment of a loan.
degree	a position or title awarded in recognition of completion of an educational course of study.
dependent	a person who is reliant upon a parent for support.

determination	a decision reached after careful consideration.
direct deposit	a way of depositing funds directly into an account without any involvement from the owner of the account.
Direct loan	a type of low interest loan offered by the DOE to help pay for the cost of college after high school.
disabled	physically or mentally impaired.
disbursement	the paying out of funds to those entitled to them.
discharge	to have the balance of a loan discarded.
disqualify	to make unable to qualify.
Doctorate degree	an advanced degree of higher learning awarded in recognition of completion of coursework in a particular field.
DOE	Department of Education. A branch of the federal government that deals with student loans.
EFC	Expected Family Contribution. A calculation figure used to express the amount of need a student has, based on their family's contribution.
eligible	able, or meeting the criteria, to receive or participate.
enroll	to enlist in classes.
entry test	a test given to access the aptitude in a specific area at the beginning of a semester.
ESL	English as a Second Language. ESL classes are designed to help students who have difficulty speaking, reading, and writing the English language.
exit interview	a study of the original terms about the repayment of a student loan.

expense	something that costs you money.
facility	a building or structure designed for a specific purpose.
FAFSA	Free Application for Federal Student Aid. The application that a student completes to determine what benefits may be available to him/her to attend college.
FDSLP	Federal Direct Student Loan Program. A loan program that offers Direct loans.
federal	of the U.S. government.
fee	a cost associated with something.
FFELP	Federal Family Education Loan Program. A program that offers federal loans using private funds from commercial lenders.
field	A specific area of study.
financial aid	Aid offered to students to attend school.
fine	a cost associated with a violation.
forbearance	a state in which a borrower requests postponement of repayment of a loan due to a hardship.
forgiveness	the discharging, or nullifying, of a loan balance.
fraud	the actual of intentionally deceiving by providing false information.
full-time	an enrollment status consisting of 12 units or more.
funds	money.
garnishment	the act of having one's income taken for repayment of a debt.
GED	General Education Diploma. A diploma awarded after successfully completing the

	necessary requirements of general education.
general education	Basic education, including reading, math, writing, history, and other areas of study usually learned from grades K through 12.
GMAT	General Management Admission Test. A test that is administered as an entry exam to a Business program, such as to receive an MBA.
goal	a desired state, which one hopes to achieve.
government	a body that rules, runs, or administers a population.
GPA	Grade Point Average. An average score of a student's grades used to indicate a student's academic ability.
grace period	a period of time before a loan goes into repayment.
graduate	a person who has graduated.
graduation check	a check performed on a student's record to ensure the student has met graduation requirements.
graduate student	A student completing coursework at the Master's degree level.
grant	funds awarded to a student that do not have to be repaid.
GRE	Graduate Record Examination. A test that is used as an admission requirement for many graduate programs.
half-time	an enrollment status consisting of at least 6 units.
hardship	troubles that interfere with one's ability to follow through on something.
high school	a level of school that comes after junior high and before college.

household	a combination of all people living with you.
income	the amount of money one makes.
independent	a status which defines a student as being self-sufficient and not relying on parents.
institution	a structure of social order that governs the behavior of a set of individuals.
instructor	a teacher that instructs a given lesson.
interest	money that is owed based on a given rate of a loan.
international	of or coming from a foreign land.
internship	an opportunity to work in an environment related to his/her field of study for experience.
ISEE	Independent School Entrance Exam. An exam used to assess aptitude for entering a private school.
itemize	to list individually each item.
job	an arrangement in which a person is employed to perform a service for an hourly wage.
junior college	a college that students attend after high school prior to going to a university.
legal	governed by federal or state law.
lender	an cntity that loans money.
limit	a point at which the maximum amount of funds a student can borrow is reached.
loan	an amount of money borrowed by a person or entity that must be repaid.
LSAT	Law School Admission Test. A test administered to assess a student's aptitude for entering law school.

major	a degree objective consisting of a course of study in a particular area.
married	a legal term indicating one's status of being married.
Master's degree	a degree of higher learning achieved after achieving a Bachelor's degree.
MCAT	Medical College Admission Test. A test designed to assess a student's aptitude prior to entering a medical college.
minor	a person under the age of 16.
MSAT	Multiple Subjects Assessment Test. A test designed to assess a student's aptitude on multiple subjects.
NSLDS	National Student Loan Data System. A database of student loan information.
objective	a choice or goal that a student hopes to achieve.
obligated	responsible for fulfilling or achieving.
occupation	a field of employment in which one works.
ombudsman	a person who serves as an intermediary between an organization and a student.
orientation	a session at the beginning of school that new students attend in order to learn about college.
originator	the creator or founder of a loan.
orphan	a legal term used to describe a ward of the court or a child without parents.
paid	no longer a debt to be settled.
parent	the owner or caregiver of a child.
paycheck	a check received by a person on a regular basis for performing a job.

Pell grant	a federal grant awarded to eligible students that does not have to be repaid.
Perkins loan	a low interest loan offered to students to pay for post-secondary education.
permit	a ticket, or decal, that gives one the right to park on campus.
philanthropy	the donating of money by a wealthy person or entity to a cause.
PLUS loan	a type of loan offered to parents to pay for educational expenses of the children.
post graduate	a level or academic achievement in which a person has completed a master's degree and is pursuing a doctorate level degree.
postpone	prolonging repayment of a loan.
preparatory test	a test designed to measure a student's aptitude before entering a college or degree program.
prerequisite	something that is required prior to.
principle	the original amount of a loan, which interest is added onto.
private lender	a lender not affiliated with the federal government.
professional	someone who is of a vocation that requires specialized educational training.
program	a course of study designed to produce a certain degree or education.
promissory note	a legal document that explains the details of a contract, such as repayment terms of a student loan.
provision	a clause in a legal document that stipulates a particular matter.
PSAT	Preliminary Scholastic Aptitude Test. Offered by the National Merit Scholarship Program, this test is taken by students prior to 12th grade in high school to assess them to would be scholarships before entering college.

PSLF	Public Service Loan Forgiveness. A program designed to forgive the balance of your student loan after completion of 120 on time payments and employment as a public service employee.
quarter	a semester based on quarter system.
receipt	to have received, or a document that serves as record of payment.
record	an accumulation of data indicating a student's academic achievement, or payment history.
reimbursement	money that is refunded after all adjustments have been made.
repayment	making payment that is due on a loan.
requirement	an element that is necessary in order to continue.
residency	a status that indicates your legal place of residence.
responsibility	an obligation to follow through on something.
room & board	quarters that provide shelter and sustenance.
SAT	Scholastic Aptitude Test. A test given prior to leaving high school to measure a student's aptitude in certain areas.
savings & loan	a financial institution that accepts savings deposits and makes mortgage and other loans.
scholarship	an award, either monetary or other, based on various criteria granted to students who apply for them.
school	an institution whose purpose is to teach.
score	a figure discerned after calculating how well a student performed on a test.

semester	a segment of an academic calendar year during which classes are held.
session	a time during which school is active.
SID	Student Identification. A card that contains a student's I.D. number and a photo identifying the student.
single	a legal status characterized by being unmarried.
Social Security Number	a nine-digit number designated to U.S. citizens by the government for tax purposes.
spouse	a marriage partner.
Stafford loan	a form of loan offered by the federal government to help undergraduate and graduate students pay for their education.
status	a condition, state, or situation.
stipend	a form of salary for work performed that would normally be unpaid, such as for an internship.
student	one who attends school to receive an education.
Student Union	an organization at a school that offers services to students.
study	engage in learning.
subsidized	the interest on a loan is paid by the government while you are in school.
term	a period of repayment of a loan.
test	a battery of questions completed by a student to measure aptitude.
tier	a level or area or hierarchy.
TOEFL	Test of English as a Foreign Language. A test that measures the ability of a person to use and understand English in an academic

	setting.
TPD	Total and Permanent Disability. A person is completely and permanently disabled.
tract	an area of study.
transcript	a record of a student's academic progress containing classes taken and grades earned, as well as bestowed titles and degrees, from a particular school.
tuition	the cost of attending school.
tutor	a person who helps a student to better understand their course material.
undergraduate	an educational level in which a student is working on a bachelor's degree.
units	a denomination of the value of an educational course.
university	an educational institution that offers more advanced facilities than a junior college and offers undergraduate and graduate degrees.
unsubsidized	the interest on a student loan is not paid by the government while the student is in school.
veteran	a person who had experience over a long period of time in a particular field, such as the military.
voucher	a tender substituted as a form of payment.
waiver	a document stating that fees do not have to be paid by the student.
ward of state	court ordered custody of a child to the state.
work study	a form of financial aid in which a student performs a job and receives payment for it.

Websites

benefits.va.gov/benefits/vonapp.asp

edupass.org

fafsa.gov

nafsa.org

nsldsfap.ed.gov

studentaid.gov

va.gov

References

CAL GRANT "What It Is and How to Apply." Victorville, CA: Victor Valley College, 2010. Print.

"Dedicated to Helping International Students." NAFSA. Washington, DC: NAFSA, 22 July 2011. NAFSA.org. Web.

"Direct Subsidized and Direct Unsubsidized Loans." Federal Student Aid. https://studentaid.gov. Web. 15 Feb. 2025.

"Edupass! The Smart Guide to Studying in the USA." Edupass! Financial Aid for International Students. Mark Kantrowitz, 2016. http://edupass.org/finaid/loans.phtml. Web. 10 Sept. 2016.

Information Sheet: Undergraduate. Services...To Students with Disabilities. San Bernardino, CA: California State University San Bernardino, 29 Apr. 2011. Flyer.

"National tests and prep courses." U.S. Dept. of Veterans Affairs. VA.gov. https://va.gov/education/about-gi-bill-benefits/how-to-use-benefits/national-tests/#how-do-i-get-paid-back-for-pre Web 24 Jan. 2025.

Ryan, Greg. Financial Aid and You: "Working Together for Student Success." Victorville, CA: Victor Valley College, June 2010. Pamphlet.

"Title IV Programs." Federal Student Aid. n.d. http://studentaid.gov//about/title4_programs.html. Web. 7 May 2012.

VVC Flyer. Flyer has no title. Victor Valley College, n.d. Victorville, CA. Contains information about the enrollment process and instructions for applying for financial aid.

Made in United States
Cleveland, OH
04 November 2026

47645299R00058